Joys

Poems (1888-1889)

Läszt Sich Kaum die Wonne fassen
– JOHAN WOLFGANG, GŒTHE.

Francis Vielé-Griffin

Translated By Richard Robinson

Sunny Lou Publishing Company
Portland, Oregon, USA
http://www.sunnyloupublishing.com

2nd Edition Revised & Corrected: November 24, 2025
2nd Edition: February 21, 2024
Original Publication Date: February 5, 2022

ISBN: 978-1-955392-58-7

# # #

This translation from French is based on the Tresse and Stock Publishers' edition of *Joies,* Paris, 1889.

Contents

Dedication

I decked my realm with frail lilies
Like virgins and like joys;
My bright palace has fine turrets,
And I draped my skies in pale silk.

I seeded my garden with sacred flora
Like virgins and like joys,
And I got drunk on my hyacinths,
Every time you blushed, Aurora.

I sing the silly things in my soul,
Like virgins and like joys,
And I found such sweet words,
O so sweet, you must believe them.

To scent your erubescent life,
I decked my realm with frail lilies,
That the breeze singing in my turrets
Sways with each nascent dawn.

That your steps might crush with aromas,
I seeded my garden with sacred flora,
That other men don't recognize,
And we will get drunk on my hyacinths.

That your lips might blossom into a smile,
I sing the silly things in my soul;
I know things, and I tell them to you,
O, I have found such sweet words.

For the Reader

The verse is *free verse*; – which means nothing more than that the "old" Alexandrine with one or more "cæsura", with or without "rejet" or "enjambment," is abolished or put down; but – more generally – that no fixed form is considered as the necessary mold anymore for the expression of all poetic thought; that, from now on, but consciously free this time, the Poet will obey the personal rhythm that must be, without M. de Banville or any other "legislator of Parnassus" intervening; and that talent shall resplend in different ways than by the traditional or illusory "vanquished difficulties" of rhetorical poetics: – Art is not merely learnt, it recreates itself continually; it does not live by tradition, but by evolving.

– June 1889.

A Bird Was Singing

Behind my father's house, a bird was singing,
In an oak tree in the woods,
– Formerly –
A ray of sunlight ran through the thick wheat;
A butterfly floated in the azure of slow days
That the breeze fanned;
The future rose up in a mirage of towers,
That a river embraced with the snares of its detours;
It was the chateau of faithful lovers –
The bird told me so.

Behind my father's house, a bird was singing
The song of my dream;
And voice of the plain, and voice of the strand,
And voice of the woods that April excites,
The echo of the future, smiling, dissimulated:
With a young heart, the soul is a crazy serf,
And both sang
From Spring to Summer.

Behind my father's house, in an oak tree in the woods,
A bird was singing of hope and joy,
Was singing of life and its tourneys
And the lance one breaks and the lance one bends;
The laughter of the lady who espies
The vanquisher whose conquest she is;
The lady is seated in her dress of silk
And presses an amulet against her heart.

Behind my father's house, a bird was singing,
From dawn till night;
And in the evenings of solitary *ennui*
Its song haunted me;
So that by chance, I remember the scales
Of its very sweet words,

Picked up among the ferns and mosses,
And repeated them to vague ladies,
Blonde ladies, or brunettes, or redheads,
Vaporous ladies, and soulless ladies.

Behind my father's house, in an oak tree in the woods,
A bird was singing a proud song;
And in the evenings, filled with nervous agitations,
I listened to it on the sill;
They are dead, the old days of proud massacres;
Foaming from atop my will's bit, they
Have reared with the triumph of coronations,
They have sniffed at the coffin's flowers,
Aromas of catafalques – sweet and acrid –
My vanities are in the coffin.

Behind my father's house, a bird was singing.
It sings in my soul and in my heart, this evening;
I inhale at night when a censer smokes,
O rutilant gardens that birthed me,
And that I relive every hour and in all your seasons:
Joy in laughter of bright leaves by the strand,
Joy in lake-blue smiles on horizons,
Joy in prostrations of the passive plain,
Joy blossoming in shivers;
The youthful delights that were in our eyes
– Auroras and sunsets – the stars in the skies
And the portal of Life, open and spacious,
Around the time of first harvests!

Behind my father's house, in an oak tree in the woods,
Behind my father's house, a bird was singing
In the allegro music of flutes and hautboys,
In the music that vaunted you,
You, my Dream and my Cross;
Do you know how greatly life was languishing in the evenings,
Do you know how far my soul followed you,
And how your shadow tempted it

Near the Chateau of Love that the bird was singing
In an oak tree in the woods?
– Formerly. –

Through the Rose Garden

Through the fresh-blown rose garden,
Through the pallid willow bosque,
To the edge of the fishponds, in the pink dawn,
Along the lakes where the reed bends,
To the sound of a trilled song,
As far as the sun-filled plain!

Over the slow river's course
Grasses are scattered green or russet,
Oscillating gently,
Over the slow river's course
Grasses are scattered beside the mosses.

No sound but the distant rolling of carts,
No fear but that of an interrupted dream;
And no regret for what one could not do
– A distant rolling of carts –

The azure in the distance where the poplars stand
Rigid and light beside the old canal –
Ah! what familiar beings this landscape has,
How everything is gentle and normal.

The grass is taller, in this way, for my bent head,
Than the hills turning blue in the distance;
And everything in life is similar, isn't it,
Foolish soul attached to your shadow,
O you who follow yourself step by step,
Bent over yourself,
Life is like that, isn't it?

Round Dance

April has died of love and our souls are old
– The roses, dead, are trampled –
Along the clear river course, in variegated bands,
The banks unfold: the dream of vigils
Has seen life pass, strewn over mad plains,
Sleepy villages, cupola'd towns,
Hills, forests, and grey-hued willows.

Which hours among the dead were ours –
Could anyone know, in the chasm where,
One by one, the walls of our jubilant chateaus fell,
To discern the ruby of the vault amid the rubble,
And all our luxuries, piece by piece?

Roses that our dances trod on
– Petals in the dead leaves of the route,
Twice withered at the forlorn site, –
Roses you pretexted with such sweet gestures?
And no one, not even I, cares for your remains.

> *On the* Pont du Nord *a dance is given,*
> *On the* Pont du Nord *a dance is given.*

O music of laughter and steps and gowns,
And the fine clicking of a fan that conceals
The smile of your whispering lips,
While a violin swoons in some andantes.

The swirl of the waltz as prelude;
Then, a whirlwind of joy, unworthy, vain, and rude,
Or prudent yet lascivious, but still, like a prude
– O the radiant body, that every glance undresses,
And no weariness subdues.

Your soul is wild, and so young, and so fair,

Your laughter is joyful and your step, a wing,
Your voice is sweeter than the laughter of a wave,
Your grace has the glory of virgins in it.

For whom will you arch your supple back,
For whom will your brow flush with inebriation,
For whom will your braid come undone
That a dream of thought might grow ponderous?
For whom, for which slave, is your necklace of love?
Who will tell you the weight of hours, in your turn?
Your grace is cadenced in every contour.

> *No, no, my child, you will not go dancing,*
> *No, no, my child, you will not go dancing.*

Your dream would be different than all these;
Your dream would be of noble hearts and souls;
Your puberty, which no man thinks to violate,
Would blush at hearing such epithalamions.

Your every drop of blood yearns for love,
Your heart is His – (your soul is fearful)
– But he has not come, nor will he, God knows!
From the shores of the past.

Your dream in vain calls him to autumn horizons;
No welcome echo surprises your modesty;
And ever the horizon; and ever, monotonous,
O the world – the world, one cannot be deceived by it.

> *Go up to your room and begin to cry,*
> *Go up to your room and begin to cry.*

Who knows if some heart
Does not die [of] your agony?
There are fierce vows:
Your soul may yield to the enjoining victor;
Your head may bow to the kiss of genius;

There are long, fierce nights of mad avowals.

And the shadows perhaps know his name:
Look at the road and see if no one walks there;
Look at the scintillating Bridge
That arches its back there;
Listen: – the waltz continues and the laughter –
On hearing it, your sobs worsen.

You know, however, that no one waits for you there,
And that your voice in vain calls out for him;
– Well do you know – you cannot fool yourself by it.

> *My sister, my sister, what have you to cry about?*
> *My sister, my sister, what have you to cry about?*

O the night, the heavy night;
Not a star –
The firmament also mourns its disaster,
O heart, and at your death no star will shine.

You will not smile but for the death of your soul;
That shadow where you languish has no concern
For a nuptial flame, and every epithalamion
Would waken the echo that sleeps far from the plain.

You will not smile but for a regret,
A regret so sweet that it is a joy,
A regret simple and noble like a minuet,
A regret of early dawn and of the sky where turns red
One aurora – the candor and modesty of your life! –
Unrealized dream, but which remains
Something beyond that mad hour
And whose hope survives and so softly cries
That the regret is sweeter than the afterlife.

Your soul is betrothed to the Same, still, still;
Your heart has scorned less handsome knights,

You have not surrendered your waist in the sonorous dance
Save to the One for whom you want your necklaces to sparkle;
Your distracted laughter and gaze, at a distance from the group,
Sought only the return of his unknown soul...
The sky clears at the song of rounds and cups.

> *Don your white gown and your golden belt!*
> *Don your white gown and your golden belt!*

Music in celebration and music on the lips
Of kisses tardily promised and stolen;
Look at you now, whiter than your white gown
Among the music and excitement.

Queen of the ball in the golden belt,
Queen of the ball with the precious necklace,
Queen of the ball, where is your knight,
Who will unfasten your golden belt?

"He will come by the river, in the first new light
"Of dawn;
"He comes to me, standing in his skiff,
"And I have put on my belt and my gown;
"Do you see him, standing in the gleam of his arms,
"He whose pure gaze has defied all charms,
"And whose soul has known no alarms?

"I have waited for you longly, gentle prince,
"My eyes have grown weary, my eyes have drowned in tears;
"O lead me to your province,
"Bear me away, the wayward daughter,
"O my gentle prince!"

> *She took three steps and behold: she has drowned,*
> *She took three steps and behold: she has drowned.*

April has died of love, and our souls grow old
– Songs of a cracked bell –

The ruination where my heart bled its slow vigils
Into the ditches, stone by stone, has rolled along;
And in the night, as if to pardon,

The bell towers of the North have begun ringing.

It snows on our hearts the ancient ages of worlds,
It snowed on our hearts the golden flowers of April;
All the wine we tasted was sweetened by other lips,
The only wine we drink is of our own fevers.

Our soul sets sail on the oceans
For the gay shores of a clear dream,
But the shipwreck at the Syrtes lay in wait:
The avid wind will reap
The glaucous plain of the sea.

The bell towers of the North have begun ringing.

The wind howls, the wind is from Batz and Ouessant;
The world is empty, and you may die –
The sand forgets a passerby's step
Whether he walks or runs;
And some hasten and some tarry to wonder
Along the way;
O you, who go, listen, listen:

The bells of the North have begun ringing.
The bells of the North have begun ringing.

May Flower

The May flower,
All murmuring with mad bees,
Blossoms and smiles,
And is dappled with corollas.

"What were you dreaming last summer
Amidst the golden harvests?"
– "A dream that must be renounced
And that sheds its petals into the hollow of footpaths,
A foolish, puerile dream, so fragile
That joy scintillates through it,
Like a web on some wood horsetail
Filtering the sun that threads through it
And that even the breeze entangles,
Puerile snare and puerile
Pitfall where no wing is caught!"

The May flower trembles while whirling around,
Like a maiden enamored with being in the world
For this alone that she is blonde.

"And all that winter of *ennui*, without a smile;
O the slow, the slow vigils!"
– "Now all is like a lyre's song;
The men playful, the women teased;
Each one acting as naughty as he can be;
The girls marvel at being marveled at
And all is round which turns and veers.

Now all that was sadness is passed;
Enter my soul and laugh in my heart"
– "Now all that was sorrow is passed,
Kiss my cheek and play with my tresses;

See: I have more than joy for you on this one lip

Than all those have for others."
– "See: I have love, that no heart is weaned of."
– "See: I have life – O, what a dream is ours!"

The May flower quivers under the weight of gay garlands;
Another couple, another twist at the top;
Flowers upon flowers! May one ravage the land,
May one join in the round, may the fête never stop:
The poet has enough tears for the lot of us.

Speak to Me

Give me the breeze in the smiling leaves,
And the wind running down dusty ways,
And the salutary aroma of pious floras,
All yesterdays and todays;

Give me the poem of grave rivers,
The placid look of forgotten lakes,
The untranslated dream of suave hours
Where our regrets are palliated;

Give me the Ocean that one hears at night
– On nights of closed eyes or veiled stars –
Give me the confession of your soul
And the sound of your spoken dreams;

Speak to me in the true range of your voice
– No matter to me, at present, the banal victory:
I have dreamt of mortal things for twenty years,
And the Shadow has swaddled me in its glory.

You So Bright

"You, so bright and so golden-blonde and so female,
You, all the dream of springtime nights,
You, gracious like a flame
And svelte and frail in soul and body,
Gay and light like banners;
And your smile soaring like a scale
Through the clearings in an echo –"

"You, my pride all proud,
You, the sole goal, sole way, and sole end,
You, by whom alone I dream of being culled,
You, my poem and my thirst and my hunger,
What evening has fallen, what hour has grown old?"

"Me, I take off toward golden rivers,
Rolling from the South toward hyperborean plains;
Quester of unknown sources
I have followed the shore of golden flowers:
The winds pushed me to an encounter with the waves
And I no longer heard my own sobs;
By the span of my soaring sails
I followed the shore to an encounter with the waves."

"I have gone out in the laughter of the breezes
By the June orchard all bejeweled with cherries,
In the flowers' aroma and the song of cedars
By a vague path propitious to mistakes,
All sliding and silent through the tall cedars:
I sounded my way well into the grey hours."

"Me, I came upon a place that a mountain harbors,
Under a cold and grey sky whose sadness spreads,
I felt tired for the fight and dreamless;
I ran aground, left my barque, and scrambled up the bank
And I walked through the country,

At dawn, when the moon rises."

"Here is the crossroad – All roads meet here –
Dangers' path leads into fatal circuits:
For the last time before they separate
Our hearts beat as one under the nights' dream."

"See, my pride grows weak and I am feeble in the shade..."

"See my pudor die and give itself and want you..."

"... It seems that a star, see! vacillates and darkens..."

"... Listen: the forest, over there in the distance, stirs..."

Some Birds Came

Some birds came to tell you
That I espied you under the mauve lilacs,
For you turned red in a smile
And hid your eyes in your tawny rings of hair
And you were taken with laughter.

Some flowers promised you something,
For you spoke to them as one admonishes,
Now here you are turning pink
While pulling their petals with so pretty a gesture
That it tells the reason for it.

The sea where your gaze goes in skiffs
Tells you, it too: "Your good fortune rubs shoulders with you";
Turning round, how is it you grow fearful and fail
To see me, there, very close by, under the frail lilacs
– The sea, or the flowers, or the martins,
Or your very own soul, subtle in its joy?

In a Wood Calm and Fresh

In a wood calm and fresh
Where no round is danced
Save my mottled thoughts
Wild mint abounds;
I made many a dream come true there
Far from the world.

The gentle wood, the saintly forest,
With its familiar trees,
Its copses that one could not
Count the branches of, in the thousands;
Sitting in the hospitable shade
I munch on an ivy leaf,
Hearing the poplars whisper,
When a pallid shiver runs,
Through their scattered greenery:

> "Your laugh is dear to the echo even,
> Which re-tells it among the elms,
> And it is in this way that I love you
> And will tell your words again;
> Your shade is fresh to the grey grass,
> Your soft weight rejoices the moss,
> Thus my soul, it too has sat
> In the shade of your sweet soul."

It rains on the blossoming mosses
In fat droplets of sunlight;
The hours spread throughout the prairies
And the air is heavy with sleep;
Across the path in an arch,
Through the ogive of branches,
It planes atimes, a cloud with white wings;
Over there, on the horizon of the shores,
The slowness of the heaviest clouds

Stood out like a patriarch,
With grave and sage dreams;
The blackbird's song is no longer heard,
A sound comes from the beaches:

> "It is something to be
> So insouciant while elsewhere crashes,
> Avid and crazy, the sea of Life;
> Your voice is a wave, too,
> Your voice which swells and pearls,
> Thus, softly and without words."

The hours pass smiling or silent
And the shade approaches the thick trunk of the ilexes,
That bathe in the soft light;
The rays fall obliquely, slowly,
And, under the breeze, the listening leaves
Whisper from moment to moment
A name that never varies:

> "In a clear song of fine love
> Your voice is married to the leaves,
> To the water dripping from the polished rock,
> To the warbling in the air, Mary,
> Your voice quietly is married;
> That shadow is violet and pink,
> You hold a coquette's flower
> In your hand which slowly drops;
> The flower is rose and violet;
> Your neck leans to the music
> That your half-closed lips tell:
> It is in this way that women dream:
> To love you thus, it is something."

The silver birches have the sveltenesses of women
Amongst the morose male pines.

The wind, sometimes mute, wanders and wishes to speak

Like a child that awakens,
Like a child that wants to speak
The wind knows only how to weep;
The wind weeps in æolian accords,
Sad enough to make one weep,
Sad like your dark shadow that approaches.

And the forest slowly grows isolate,
One walks there like an intruder at twilight.

Its august life turns back
Far from the man and his word,
Too mean for its great umbrous dream;
The woods are solemnized in the temple,
The religious woods contemplate
The mêlée where the shadows must conquer.

– O hymn of tall pines to the setting sun!

The lamentation ululates slowly and drags
Through the valley in heavy threnodic rhythms;
The leaves float and land finally;
Through the woven, shadowy copses
The shame of dying sobs;
The eternal forest agonizes forever;

Silently, the leaves pile up to rot
– In the shade, forever.

The Mild Evenings Are Withered

"The mild evenings are withered like flowers in October
– What would we say to the willows, the gorse, the lagoons? –
My soul has been made grave and sober forever;
– What would we say to the dunes?

The wind rises and approaches, discreet and silent:
My temple is fresh with its kiss;
Night – quietly, like a mother who consoles
– Rises and comes to embrace me and rock me –
What would we say to the willows?

You were my king for a flowering season,
You were the elect by your gentle words;
Did we know, when we laughed,
That we were both playing old roles?

Did I know it, me? You, did you know it?
– Now that all is grey on the nocturnal land –
With our false and quiet laughter?
What had the taciturn future told us?
What did we know?

Me, I dreamt, doubtless, of old poems,
And you, of old tales of good fortune:
'You love me?' – 'I love you!' – 'You love me!'
How old were we then to be laughing at ourselves?
What were we going to say to the dunes?
To the willows, the gorse, the lagoons?
– The moon rises in its pale haloes –
Our hearts will be dead without rancor."

The Road

"It was slow and long and feverish, the night;
The weight of hours grew heavy with darkness,
Where sometimes a sudden light flashed,
Sketching mad algebras in the sky
– But throughout space not a sound –

It was slow and gloomy and funereal, the dawn
– Shroud of a stillborn day in bloody throes –
The sun, veiled in mourning, slips away;
Along bitter and slippery roads
Teardrops fall on your dress.

It was morose and wan and sepulchral, that day,
Filled with strange, subdued and mysterious sounds.
Full like a breeze, motionless and heavy,
That suffocates the earth with its miasmas
– Behold the Land of Love –

O let it be sweet and slow and smiling, the sleep.
Amid the harsh regrowth and sharp stubble;
The crepuscule of repose summons us.
O, how long we have wandered,
You, all woman, and me, all man."

The Blue Wind from o'er the Mountains

"The blue wind from o'er the mountains makes the ash trees shiver;
At a distance from the woods a summer carillon peals;
Towards the meadows of China asters, ermine and golden,
And through the endless azure, like a song of sirens
Repeated by coral reefs,
The large, slow clouds move, swelling in carinas...

An unending murmur wells up from the pasturage:
June sings in the new wood that echos its gaiety;
Skiffs stacked with grey hay wait patiently along the bank,
The death of scythed flowers is toxic in the sap
And my lips would have collected
From yours the Apriline honey of your dream...

The hour passes gentle and quick at crepuscule;
The sun, nearly fallen, has proudly stopped
Over there, royal still; and smoke undulates
From the pyre in the West to the zenith that burns...
My eyes have watched
Your soul in your eyes when the future recedes...

The hour was such, and everything is similar and resembles itself;
The river still rolls in glimmers of Lethe.
The horizon also is still such – what does it seem like to you? –
Is it still a dream wherein we dream together?
Is there anything you regret?
The night, drunk on incense, is amorous and trembles..."

"But! Are we the same as we used to be?"

A Star

She sang at evening, for me alone and her dream,
And I took up that song again that was dying on her lips
In a kiss of love that no winter might wean;
I sang while laboring, like a goldsmith,
Winding and unwinding her tress – bright gold of the strand!

A star, on high, glimpsed through the chance
Mist of a brightening in the hibernal night,
A single star at the further reaches of the night;
A single lantern beneath gusts and showers:
And the woman's soul that my dream assumes
Grows sad that it gleamed.
The wee hours of the night weigh; efface yourself; you sully the
                                                      [shade:
My soul shuts its eyes to it, star, and feels strong;
But let her weep her somber dream,
For the hour is passed, and the year is dead:

"I saw it pass from where I was binding my sheaf,
The beautiful ship setting out for high seas,
I had seen it pass, between vessels, superb,
Along the estuary where the path is herbless,
Having come from the open sea, on the flux, in a clear sky,
Brailing the bister canvas on its mast, like
A runner who stops and collapses on the grass;
And some birds were twittering high up in the air,
And the sun was turning the acerb sand pink, over there,
And the flux overrunning in foam
As far as the beacon which, at night, lights up
And turns its light on the sky,
And as far as the dunes, grey like a fog...

– (The flux, and the ship, and the sky so clear) –
The brisk larboard wind grew cooler, by evening;
The screeching capstans have fallen silent and watch;

The flux has covered the dark side of the hulls,
The landing stage will shimmer with the lights that guard it;
– (What soul am I then, that it smiles at me yet?
That a star, on high! – the sunset was the color of bronze) –
My heart was beating for no reason, and I dreamt of following
The shadow of large vessels that set out for the North...

– (The breeze, and the penumbra, and the lanterns of the port) –
The night came, pale, with sleepless dreams
The pensive night of June when the soul is alone and vigils
Seated in the shade and which shivers and marvels;
Slow steps on the path, and I cocked an ear;
He sat down near the sill where the arbor trembles,
He told me of evenings when the sea is vermillion,
In Western lands where the sun slumbers,
And I followed him from marvel to marvel;
His voice was so gentle, and it was a joy
That filled me with a shiver so traitorous that I laughed.
He spoke to me very softly, and I didn't dare cry out
When he seized my hand through the openwork fence.
As one catches a surprised bird in the evening...

– (His voice in the shade, and his hand through the openwork fence) –

Ah! it was one evening... Who remembers:
For to live, is it not to relive forever then?
I am some dead woman, doubtless, and some dream,
With my etesian evening tale,
When the wind is mournful along the strand
– (I am some dream read in some book,
Some tale, some poem, on a dreamlike evening). –

But this time, I laughed at a word
That I still blush for... and that I hear!
– (I do not even know if I'm not crazy) –
I don't care anymore where the path leads me.
I do not know where my life drifts to:
I have lived for but one hour, and but one kiss;

I do not know where the path deviates:
All my future, in one evening, was erased.

He departed, for over there, one bitter evening;
– (Which star, on high, seen through the mist?) –
The ship went out to sea again, but without him.
– (A single star at the further reaches of the night
A single lantern in the night is lit) –
He departed down the path, one evening,
On a horse with a black head, body
White like sea foam and clouds.
He departed, one evening long ago,
Whilst the tempest raged;
He got lost in the black night
In the grey corners of my memory;
My soul is there, which he killed.

What matter to me now, having been her soul:
Time could not fade his lips on mine;
No weight of time can make me forget
– (I am the shade and echo of an epithalamic evening) –
… It was one evening, in the etesian penumbra…"

Those Hours Then

Those hours then were good to us.
Like sisters moved to pity;
Hours sweet and monotonous,
Pale and drowned in the mists,
With their pale nuns' veils.

Didn't they deserve our laughter then,
Those smiles without bitterness
For the heavy past whence we came?
Ah! dear, there are worse hours
Than those hours with misty veils.

They passed smiling
– Like nuns praying –
Bathed in opaline glimmers,
The sweet, resigned hours.

Go on, our souls are still sisters
Of the hours of grey autumn,
Whose penumbra in our hearts
Stumped our old disdains
And we no longer saw our tears.

In Memoriam

The roses leaning
Over the red-sandstone balustrades
Shed their blood petals into the rippling waves;
– The banks are utterly strewn with them –
Their folioles engarland, in passing,
Your lacustrine corollas,
Dazzling, white water lily.

I have crowned you, o pale, gentle soul,
With mortal, petalless flowers on your eyes;
But no heartfelt mourning will have sullied them,
Our loves where you had no rival,
Our loves that no one will have jeered at.

            * * *

Those were evenings of starry dreams
– *What eternal forgetfulness outrages us?* –
Dreams in rhythm with the songs of the strand,
Haunted by your bright piercing eyes,
And tears of rage.

Those were morning madnesses
– *What murderous winter withered our springtimes?* –
Silken skies and satin seas,
And the entire absoluteness of our twenty years.
And all the songs we struck up.

There was in the woods and in the meadows and on the shores
– *What a shudder we feel as if opening a tomb?* –
There was in the joy and the laughter and dreams
All the heartfelt Infinity that one discovers
In the distance, blooming in its brief hours.

            * * *

A song returns to me in the breeze each May
As in a breath from you who were sleeping,
Like your voice in naïve songs,
Silent – and forever sonorous in my soul;

An aroma in the April breeze circulates
Far and wide and it smells of the banks
And the woods in deep crepuscular mourning
And all the past that my soul returns to
Through the night and in its passive hours;

Till this evening, till this dream,
Your voice sings to me its grave music;
What fool will tell us that joy is brief?
It is eternal and sweet grief!...

The roses leaning
Over the red-sandstone balustrades
Dispetal into the rippling waves that once beheld their beauty;
Not one field is left uncut;
Life is crumbling, lustrum after lustrum;
What flower and what hour shall be immortal!

Aubade

Follow at dawn, golden and tawny,
The grassy path running to the edge,
Gay for a rememorated hour,
Without dreaming of crowned glory.
– (Life exults in unknown joy.) –

Do not think on the future;
No wills are masters of it.
Live, this listless day, on memories;
Glory, it may come,
But it will not be worth your distresses,
– (The pond glistens around the Menhir.) –

If your soul fills and overflows,
It is that your life is forever full;
If, heavy in ears, the harvest bends over,
Your sorrows had inseminated them.
– (What soul turns pale in the white dawn?) –

Summer laughs at you, Love wraps you
In the light mantle of its wings;
The auroral shiver embraces you
In a unison of chanterelles.
– (What swan in the dawn sings and bleeds?)

By the Sea

My heart exits the Sea and is resorbed by it...

Nothing in the offshore breeze wherein to dream of your terrace:
Not a petal, nor a butterfly – nor even a wing; –
Not a scent of the orchard in the sea spray that dispels it,
Nor even a sound of irreal foliage
In the monotone and tenacious knell
That clamors – are you dead then? – in the undertow at Frehel.

Near the large, distraught, and tragic cross,
Whose naked gibbet I dressed with our love,
I wept by the sea that sobbed in response,
Like your voice, perhaps, and like your heavy heart;
Beyond the ocean that moans its silent dream,
I watched for your response.

… The grass is gayer in the hollow of our ravines, – clearly –;
Our lake is bluer – for it is early summer;
The island sleeps at anchor just as it was,
And the path of the rock is cheerful under its vault,
And its doorsill that your steps fêted is in bloom
And its echo that your voice fêted is moved!...

– My soul is dissolved in a sea of tears,
My heart – into the sea I have cast it!

       * * *

The garden was rustling by the doorstep,
The birds flying from the porch;
The shade of a beech tree, from the doorstep,
Lay about in violet mourning;
Around a rosebush, flame pink,
Vibrated some bees in a halo;
It was the Land of wonders

That we contemplated from the porch
– A dream of future vigils. –

Along the bushes blooming in amber,
Near the rocks grey like December,
Under the weight of your hair you arch your back,
With your cloud of hair, so heavy
With its golden thurible where amber resins burned...
What had become of our love?
– If toward my desires you arch your back,
Beyond the ocean that moans its muted dreams,
Nothing will exist of our love!...

If I had thought to tell you,
"That there are cornflowers in your eyes,
And roses in your smile
And ears of grain in your hair."
And, for all that, if I thought to tell you:
"That life is sweet for him who wants it,
That in every look a look is mirrored,
That in every voice an echo is stirred;"
But could I know – the madness! –
For what pain I was loving you
And that life is sad and forgets,
And that time dies forever...

We drifted, for hours, along the banks
Where the branches tendered their shade,
And sometimes joined into ogives
As in somber cathedrals;
And some current led us,
Wither it would, slowly, where the creek slumbers;
And that water lily at my peril given,
And the laughter in a smile that was your response...
At what hour was eternity ringing?
For here I am still listening to it
Beyond the ocean that moans with muted dreams,
On the lookout for your response.

* * *

My soul drowns at sea
My heart bleeds in the morose waves...

Where do you cull the jasmine?
Where do you pick the roses?
Do you know when joy will reflourish?
– My heart has lost its way,
My soul drowns at sea –

I wept by the sea that surges and unfurls,
And, fool, I reached out my hand to you,
Dream that dissolves you in vapors faraway,
As collapses, dying, a wave that unfurls;
Dream of dawn that evaporated at morning,
Like, soaring, a blackbird's song that fades;
Love's defunct dream, haunting every tomorrow;
As, gently retracted, a hand
Leaves the imprint of a pearl
Indelible on the fingers that clutched it in vain.

I wept by the sea that sobs and unfurls.

She Who Passes

She who passes smiled at me
– The azure is paler and the air is pink –
She who passes without a pause,
Vaguely tender like a Thing,
Like a stream, like a flowering meadow
– She who passes smiled at me. –

All is joy, and all prays and sings
– She who passes shined. –
The Day before yesterday is pardoned,
The Mass of love sounded
With the bellflowers of the prairie:
She who passes shined.

Nothing remains of the day or the hour:
She who passes smiled, beaming;
My soul flutters through the furrows
With the butterflies and breezes,
I am the day itself that flowers and sings.
– She who passes smiled, beaming. –

With a little blonde gaiety,
In a beam by the road that climbs;
With a little of your laughter – (a wave
        That surges and flurries!) –
With, o, your sweet laughter when my dream
Fallen from its old Olympus melts
        And that weeps for joy;
With the froufrou of a skirt – (a wing!) –
With the sparkle from your eyes – (o beams!) –
Life is easy and life is beautiful
And my soul in carillons sings.

It Was an Evening of Faëries

It was an evening of faëries,
Of enribboned vapors,
Of tender marrow flowers in the prairies,
In the finest of your years.

And you said – echo of my deep soul, –
Beneath the aureole that crowns you blonde
And in the rhythmic rustling of silk:
"All is sad for joy;
What mourning fills the world?
Everything grows sad with joys."

And I responded to you, on that evening of faëries
And enribboned vapors:
"In the heavy estival scent of the prairies,
Second after second,
The finest of your years falls like leaves,
A mourning of love is on the world
With every hour sounded."

Round

Where is the Marguerite,
O ware, o ware, o ware,
Where is the Marguerite,
O ware, her chevalier?

She is in her chateau of flowers and arbors,
– Her grey eyes are lost in distant mists –
Quietly sad with the dream of young women,
Blonde in the morning.

She is in her chateau with its lithe Turrets,
On the emblossomed terraces;
Where the hours are heavy that seem easy,
Slow and heavy like the years.
Slow and so wrongly praised,
Slow and languidly sounded.

She is in her chateau which an oak grove isolates
Looming above hamlets beneath lofty towers
And o'er which a flock passes, soaring into the beyond;
She evokes in an echo of distant songs
Where a heart bathed in tears wept
And joyful in its pain,
Some Minstrel laureate:

"Do you know an hour wherein neither heart
Nor soul is afflicted, weary finally of waiting?
Are you there? Where your desire harbors
In the shadows that fall silent and tender?..."

Where is, the Marguerite,
O ware, o ware, o ware,
Where is, the Marguerite,
O ware, your chevalier?

* * *

Where is the Marguerite,
O ware, o ware, o ware,
Where is the Marguerite,
O ware, her chevalier?

She is in her orchard under the snow-covered apple trees,
Light, and as her April dream lightens,
Her dream where Love passes in cortège
– And the cloth on the grass dazzles in the sun –

She is in her orchard, wholly troubled
By the toxins that April has flourished on the hedge
– It shivers in the grasses, a quivering song –
And her happiness soars in vermillion laughter.

She is in her fragrant orchard that swarms
And buzzes and murmurs, the enchanter;

Pink with vague joy, drunk with the true Poem,
Half distrustful of the oracle of a flower,
But believing above all what her lover told her
The candle consecrated to the Chandler.

– She laughs to herself
And watches the road and shelters her eyes...

Where is, the Marguerite,
O ware, o ware, o ware,
Where is, the Marguerite,
O ware, your chevalier?

* * *

Where is the Marguerite,
O ware, o ware, o ware,
Where is the Marguerite,

O ware, her chevalier?

She is in her convent, who prays and weeps;
She is on her knees and hour follows upon hour;
She is in her convent, who prays and weeps;

She prays in the penumbra of the lamplight
And dreams of the lover from the marvelous City,
Of the handsome Christ, whom she is the mourner of,

She is in her cellule, who weeps and prays,
Beautiful, and who offers herself to the God of her choice,
Strewing with flowers which her soul is teeming with
The old way of the Cross.

Like a seabird, wings outspread,
Her soul is borne on the organ's storm
And planes, lost in a haze of incense,
Weary, swooning and abandoning in offerings
To the God of her choice, the entirety of her mad soul.

Her soul is transported by the organ's storm
Drunk with a credulous faith in vague miracles
– The dazzling monstrance radiates its prestiges
Over the bending priests, with their gold pieces, and their pride
– With all her soul, she is seized by vertigoes.

And her mind of a girl is leagued against her
– She is lost, she is the neophyte.

> *Where is the Marguerite,*
> *O ware, o ware, o ware,*
> *Where is the Marguerite?*

She is in her chateau, heart weary and fatigued,
She is in her hamlet, heart childish and gay,
She is in her grave, let us strew it with lily of the valley.

O ware, the Marguerite.

Epithalamion

April kissed your brow and stands in wonder,
Pale in the reflection of its bright jonquil,
When, with all your being, your expression awakens
Alone in the joyous surprise of its mysteries;
It passes and shines on you with radiant regret
Near the harvested flowers o'erflowing their basket.

May which came to the edge of the strand
Trampling the snow of the withered peach trees,
Sings to you who was dreaming in the meadow;
Yes, while your soul is still bruised by it,
Knowing your body's unknown Beauty,
And that your heart dreamt of the Lover-Faëry.

June leant over you, who was weeping, and took you
And named you, this evening, queen of its pale night:
Your red lips were, it said, cherries.
Your cheek was the orchard's fatal peach;
Then it left before dawn, leaving you surprised
– And the pain of loving sat down on your doorstep. –

July kisses your brow, as did April in passing,
And as it sings for you, like May, its several phrases,
As did June, since the evening of your regret, it makes
The night tender amidst the fresh welcome of the corollas;
The scythe of haymakings had not granted grace
To the pale lily that, fallen, an archangel gathers.

One Winter Evening

Pallor of virgins, candor of dawns,
Efflorescence of lilies and roses,
Down of swans in white robes,
Laughter of lips forever closed.

The lake grows dark in the whitenesses surrounding it
– Like a white gauze casting a shadow over a girl; –
The snow, in prodigious flocs, scatters
And revolves around the pine trees that moan;
The crazed weathervane gyrates,
The canopies lament.

Fall, o ashes of bygone years
Dead with my smile on their lips.
Folioles of our wilted gardens
In the winds of summer, in the suns of our fevers;
Sand of struck hours.

Hesitant, it passes and re-passes
In its dances outside my half-open window;
– Funereal waltzes without a musician.
Silent and fantastic in their cadences
Whose concordances vibrate in my being;
The wind dies down – and all is fine;

In my soul, where an autumn drops its leaves,
Spin round, o monotonous snow;
Cover the road, and may no step be heard
Until a silence that surprises me.

Behold an entire day as I watch it
Across the plain, where the hedge is scarcely a ripple,
Running in flurries of mist
To the rigid forest;
Until night, when a penumbra lingers,

And no star shines in the sky.

Peace in our hearts and a truce in our lives:
The hour has come when our dreams come alive;
There is no more trace of the paths we took;
Look, the poem vanishes from the book,
All our past is enshrouded in rime.

Fly, dust from the roads full of shadows,
Nocturnal spray shot up from dead seas;
Rain, crazy dead stars,
– Deserted is the porch and closed are the doors –
North wind howl in the terebinths,
Snow, o snow! through the somber night.

They Have Been Achieved, All Our Crazy Plans

They have been achieved, all our crazy plans:
My dream and your dream, the same – the same;
And every day – o the days were light,
And the evenings sweet, and the nights supreme;
Every unmitigated dream;
Everything that makes poems sweet;
Every scattered joy that troubles
– And that every soul, one evening, was afraid of. –

> *The violet doubles, doubles,*
> *The violet will double.*

I weaved rug from the flowers fit for a queen
For Her feet – roses among the lilies,
And among the roses by the tonne pale lilies:
Blue and blue-tinted in their veins – Her troubles;
I draped the throne in trembling folds
Of floral-printed fabrics – (garlands and chains) –
That Her flesh might sing of my fulfilled vows
Dazzling in the ebony panels
Of her joy – (o rose) – that trembles and that troubles
The Soul that wept too long for her.

> *The violet doubles, doubles,*
> *The violet will double.*

Then, I spent many days waiting for Her.
Not knowing what Queen was supposed to come;
With the pretense of surprising Her
And the delusion also of retaining Her;
My love becoming totally humble and so tender:
"What harm could come of it?"
And at night, often, I thought I heard Her

Singing the song that must not end
– O, I shivered in the expectation that troubles
Every soul that is too often deceived.

> *The violet doubles, doubles,*
> *The violet will double.*

But on that day of culling, the underbrush, the laughter;
And the berry in dark purple at our fingertips;
The source: I drink of it and you gaze at yourself.
Not blonde, not brunette, not tawny brown: all three –
So joyous, so much the queen of me, your empires.
– And me, your subjects, so jealous of my rights;
And you who walked, as if to the rhythm of
The Graian Graces of yesteryear:
My heart panted with the hope that troubles
And with the exquisite doubt of what will be.

> *The violet doubles, doubles,*
> *The violet will double.*

My hours, yours – the same hours, –
Your desires, mine – the same forever, –
All the tears that I weep and that you weep
Fall with dew into the garden of Love:
From the dismal emptiness of old demesnes,
From tumultuous and deafening silences,
From buried hatreds and old delusions,
The lilies and roses of Love are born
One evening of feverish joy and that troubles
The soul that for so long wept over itself.

> *The violet doubles, doubles,*
> *The violet will double.*

O our vernal days!
O our winters, and the fires, and the lamp!
All the hatreds assassinated

With our well-tempered laughter;
All the sorrows pardoned:
The old Past – the grotesque stamp,
With its hastily scribbled rhymes,
Burns in the hearth where the flame climbs;
A silence falls that nothing further troubles,
And your cheek blushed when my lips brushed it.

> *The violet doubles, doubles,*
> *The violet will double.*

Other Books by the Publisher

Fanchette's Pretty Little Foot by Restif de La Bretonne

Je M'Accuse... by Léon Bloy

My Hospitals & My Prisons by Paul Verlaine

Salvation Through the Jews by Léon Bloy

Words of a Demolitions Contractor by Léon Bloy

Cellulely by Paul Verlaine

Ecclesiastical Laurels by Jacques Rochette de la Morlière

Flowers of Bitumen by Émile Goudeau

Songs for Her & Odes in Her Honor by Paul Verlaine

On Huysmans' Tomb by Léon Bloy

Ten Years a Bohemian by Émile Goudeau

The Soul of Napoleon by Léon Bloy

Blood of the Poor by Léon Bloy

Joan of Arc and Germany by Léon Bloy

Theresa the Philosopher & The Carmelite Extern Nun by Marquis d'Argens & Anne-Gabriel Meusnier de Querlon

A Platonic Love by Paul Alexis

Two Novellas: Francine Cloarec's Funeral and Benjamin Rozes by Léon Hennique

www.ingramcontent.com/pod-product-compliance
Lightning Source LLC
Chambersburg PA
CBHW031257120626
46545CB00007B/2860